A NOTE TO PARENTS

When your children are ready to "step into reading," giving them the right books is as crucial as giving them the right food to eat. **Step into Reading Books** present exciting stories and information reinforced with lively, colorful illustrations that make learning to read fun, satisfying, and worthwhile. They are priced so that acquiring an entire library of them is affordable. And they are beginning readers with a difference—they're written on five levels.

Early Step into Reading Books are designed for brand-new readers, with large type and only one or two lines of very simple text per page. **Step 1 Books** feature the same easy-to-read type as the Early Step into Reading Books, but with more words per page. **Step 2 Books** are both longer and slightly more difficult, while **Step 3 Books** introduce readers to paragraphs and fully developed plot lines. **Step 4 Books** offer exciting nonfiction for the increasingly independent reader.

The grade levels assigned to the five steps—preschool through kindergarten for the Early Books, preschool through grade 1 for Step 1, grades 1 through 3 for Step 2, grades 2 through 3 for Step 3, and grades 2 through 4 for Step 4—are intended only as guides. Some children move through all five steps very rapidly; others climb the steps over a period of several years. Either way, these books will help your child "step into reading" in style!

For Marian Reiner, with thanks
—M.K.

For my wife, Sachi, and my two daughters, Shaina and Tarah
—C.S.

With grateful acknowledgment to Scott Rector,
of the Eleanor Roosevelt National Historic Site in Hyde Park, New York,
for his time and expertise in reviewing this book.

Text copyright © 1999 by Monica Kulling. Illustrations copyright © 1999 by Cliff Spohn.
All rights reserved under International and Pan-American Copyright Conventions.
Published in the United States by Random House, Inc., New York, and simultaneously
in Canada by Random House of Canada Limited, Toronto.
PHOTO CREDITS: AP/Wide World Photos: pp. 27, 37, 40, 48; Corbis-Bettmann: pp. 3, 26.

www.randomhouse.com/kids

Library of Congress Cataloging-in-Publication Data
Kulling, Monica. Eleanor everywhere : the life of Eleanor Roosevelt / by Monica Kulling.
p. cm. — (Step into reading. A step 4 book)
SUMMARY: Profiles the first wife of a president to have a public life and career of her own,
devoted to helping others and working for peace.
ISBN 0-679-88996-5 (pbk.) — ISBN 0-679-98996-X (lib. bdg.) 1. Roosevelt, Eleanor, 1884-1962—
Juvenile literature. 2. Presidents' spouses—United States—Biography—Juvenile literature.
[1. Roosevelt, Eleanor, 1884-1962. 2. First ladies. 3. Women—Biography.]
I. Title. II. Series: Step into reading. Step 4 book.
E807.1.K85 1999 973.917'092—dc21[B] 98-19105

Printed in the United States of America 10 9 8 7 6 5 4 3 2 1

STEP INTO READING is a registered trademark of Random House, Inc.

Step into Reading®

ELEANOR EVERYWHERE

The *Life* of Eleanor Roosevelt

By Monica Kulling
Illustrated by Cliff Spohn

A Step 4 Book

Random House 🏠 New York

1
Lonely Eleanor

The summer of 1892 was a special one for young Eleanor Roosevelt. She was spending it in Oyster Bay, Long Island, with her cousins and her favorite uncle, Theodore Roosevelt.

Eleanor's mother and her brother Elliott

were both dead. Eleanor's father was an alcoholic. He had been sent to a hospital to get better.

Eleanor missed her father very much. He loved her for who she was. She often felt that he was the only one who understood her. Eleanor's mother had thought Eleanor was too serious and old-fashioned-looking. She had jokingly called her "Granny."

Eleanor was only seven, but already her young heart was filled with pain. Playing with her cousins at Oyster Bay helped ease this pain. Eleanor also loved spending time with her Uncle Teddy. He was her father's older brother. He was fun-loving, and he adored Eleanor. One day he would become the president of the United States.

But there was a cloud in Eleanor's summer sky—Cousin Alice.

Alice teased and taunted Eleanor. At the beach, she tried to get Eleanor into the water. She knew that Eleanor couldn't swim and that she was terrified of water.

"Get in, you chicken," said Alice, pushing the frightened girl toward the water's edge. "I dare you."

Eleanor panicked. She remembered the boat trip she took with her parents when she was two. In the fog, their steamship crashed into another ship. Eleanor was dropped overboard into a waiting lifeboat. Her father's outstretched arms caught her.

Eleanor never forgot her fear and panic. In her mind, it seemed the accident had happened just yesterday. Eleanor had many fears. The fear of water was top on the list.

"Scaredy-cat! Baby!" taunted Alice. She ran into the surf. She tried to splash Eleanor.

Finally, Eleanor went back inside. She would reread her father's latest letter. It would cheer her up. In his letters, her father encouraged her to be brave. He wanted Eleanor to make him proud. He tried to comfort her by telling her that someday they would live together again.

Eleanor carried her father's letters with her all her life. She became the brave woman he wanted her to be.

Years later, Eleanor Roosevelt said: "Looking back, I see my childhood was one long battle against fear."

Eleanor conquered her fears. She grew up to be one of the most respected women in the world.

2
Eleanor Grows Up

Anna Eleanor Roosevelt was born on October 11, 1884. She was born into one of New York's richest families. She and her parents lived in an elegant townhouse in Manhattan. They had many servants. Eleanor even had a private tutor for her lessons.

Eleanor's father was handsome and

charming. Her mother was beautiful. Eleanor thought she was the most beautiful woman she had ever seen.

Looks and graceful manners were very important to Eleanor's mother. But Eleanor didn't share her mother's beauty. Her mother often told Eleanor, "You have no looks, so see to it that you have manners."

These words hurt young Eleanor deeply. She remembered them all her life.

Eleanor's life of luxury did not protect her from unhappiness. By the time she was eight, her mother and her younger brother, Elliott, had both died. Then, when she was ten, Eleanor's beloved father died.

Eleanor and her remaining brother, Hall, lived in New York City with their grandmother and several unmarried aunts and uncles.

When Eleanor turned fifteen, her grandmother enrolled her in a highly respected school for girls known as Allenswood.

"Your mother wanted you to go to boarding school in England," Grandmother Hall told her. "It is time."

Eleanor was excited at the thought of starting a new life in England.

From the beginning, she felt at home at Allenswood. The school's headmistress, Mademoiselle Souvestre, was tough but fair. She brought out the best in her students.

The school had many rules. One was that

students must always speak French. This was not a problem for Eleanor. Her tutor had always spoken to her in French. Eleanor spoke the language with ease.

While the other girls sat shyly at the first meal, Eleanor and Mademoiselle Souvestre got to know each other.

Mademoiselle Souvestre felt immediately that Eleanor was special. She wanted Eleanor to feel it too. Mademoiselle encouraged the tall girl to walk straight. She had a designer make a beautiful red dress for Eleanor. Eleanor wore this favorite dress every Sunday.

For the first time in her life, Eleanor felt accepted. The teachers liked her. Her classmates liked her. And the younger students looked up to her.

In time, Eleanor came to see herself in a new light. She might not fit her mother's idea of beauty. But she had an inner beauty. And it was beginning to shine.

Three years went by quickly. Eleanor wanted to stay at Allenswood. But her grandmother had a different plan for her. She wanted Eleanor to enter New York society. Like her mother and grandmother before her, Eleanor would have a "coming-out."

3
Eleanor Turns Eighteen

A coming-out was the custom in high society. When a girl turned eighteen, she attended fancy parties, where she was introduced to young men. It was hoped that she would soon marry.

Eleanor had been to fancy parties before. She didn't like them. She felt awkward and shy. Most of all, she worried about her looks.

"I knew I was the first girl in my mother's family who was not a belle," Eleanor said later.

But Eleanor was more of a social success than she knew. Allenswood had given her a new confidence. Eleanor had to attend a fancy formal dance at the grand Waldorf-Astoria Hotel. She dressed in an expensive gown. Her hair was done in the latest style. She wasn't the most popular girl at the party, but Eleanor had many invitations afterward. She made many new friends.

However, her new friends were different from her friends at Allenswood. They cared only about their wealth and position. They did not care about the poor.

Mademoiselle Souvestre had taught Eleanor to think of others. After she entered society, Eleanor joined the Junior League. This group of wealthy women helped poor people.

But most members of the Junior League did not want to work with the poor themselves. They were only interested in raising money. Eleanor wanted to do more.

Eleanor taught at the Rivington Street Settlement House on Manhattan's Lower East Side. She taught dance to the daughters of Jewish and Italian immigrants. The girls in her classes liked her. They often invited her to visit their homes.

Eleanor was also a member of the National Consumers League. This group worked to improve working conditions for women. Eleanor visited factories and department stores. She saw young women working long hours for little money.

Eleanor had been born into a protected world. She could have chosen to stay there. But she didn't. She cared about those who did not have as much as she did. She was interested in people from every walk of life.

4
Eleanor and Franklin

Franklin Delano Roosevelt was one of Eleanor's new friends. He was a distant cousin. She had met him when she was young. But she didn't know him very well. Now the two were getting to know each other better.

Franklin was studying at Harvard. He came to New York as often as he could to visit Eleanor. Sometimes Eleanor took him to the Rivington Street Settlement House. Franklin had also grown up in a wealthy, protected home. He had never seen people living the way these poor people lived. It was an education for him.

Eleanor and Franklin grew closer. Franklin was tall and handsome. He had a good sense of humor and loved to make Eleanor laugh. One weekend, he invited her to Boston to a football game. Eleanor traveled by train with her aunt and a cousin. In those days, young women didn't spend time alone with young men.

Franklin and Eleanor did go for one walk alone. On that walk, Franklin asked Eleanor to marry him. He felt that with her by his side, he could do anything.

Eleanor was only nineteen. She dreamed of becoming a teacher like Marie Souvestre. But wealthy women in Eleanor's day married at a young age.

Eleanor knew that Franklin loved her. And she loved him. She accepted his proposal.

Everything seemed perfect. But Franklin's mother, Sara, wasn't happy with the proposal. Franklin was her only child. She didn't want to lose him to marriage.

As a compromise, Franklin and Eleanor agreed to a long engagement. A year later, on March 17, 1905, Eleanor and Franklin were married. Eleanor's Uncle Teddy, who was now the president of the United States, walked his favorite niece down the aisle.

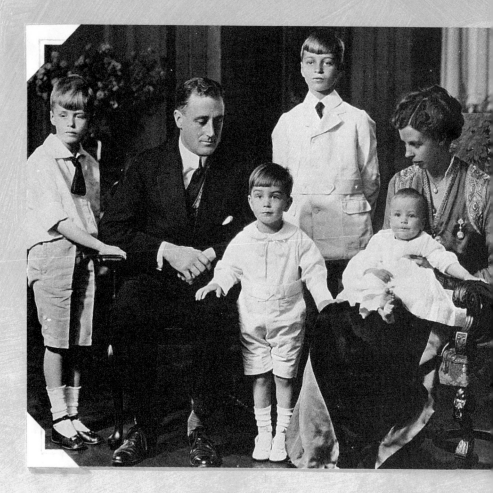

Sara gave the couple a house right next to hers. She had connecting doors built between all the floors. That way, she could visit them whenever she wanted.

Soon Eleanor and Franklin had their first child, Anna. Anna was the first of six children—one girl and five boys. But one boy, their third child, died before he was a year old.

Eleanor, Franklin, and their family.

Eleanor with her first baby, Anna.

Sara took care of everything. She hired nurses and nannies. She urged Eleanor to give up her volunteer work.

Eleanor had worked hard for her independence. Now it was slipping away. But things were changing quickly for the Roosevelts. Soon Eleanor would be doing more than she ever imagined.

5
An Unexpected Challenge

Franklin had always loved politics. He now decided to run for office. In 1910, he won a seat in the New York State Senate. The Roosevelt family moved to Albany. For the first time in her marriage, Eleanor was away from Sara Roosevelt. Now Eleanor made her own decisions. It was a freedom she enjoyed.

At the end of three years, the Roosevelts moved back to New York City. Soon President Woodrow Wilson made Franklin the assistant secretary of the navy. The family moved again—this time to Washington, D.C.

In 1920, Franklin ran for vice president. This was the same year in which women were given the right to vote. Eleanor cast her first ballot. She voted for her husband. But Franklin and the Democrats lost.

Then in 1921 tragedy struck. Franklin came down with polio. Polio was normally a childhood disease. Franklin had a high fever. His legs were paralyzed. He was told he would never walk again.

Sara wanted her son to quit politics. She wanted him to retire to the family home at Hyde Park. But Eleanor disagreed. She would not let Franklin give up. She would not let him think of himself as an invalid.

At first, Franklin could not even sit up in bed. But Eleanor's care and encouragement kept him going. Franklin worked hard at his exercises. He grew stronger. Soon he was standing with the help of metal braces. He would always need these braces. But after seven years he was walking again.

Franklin's tragedy forced Eleanor to conquer more of her fears. Franklin had always been active with their children. Now Eleanor felt she must take his place. She faced her old fear of water. She learned how to swim so she could swim with her children.

Eleanor knew Franklin wanted to return to politics. She didn't want people to forget him. So she conquered another fear—public speaking. While Franklin recovered, Eleanor made speeches at Democratic women's meetings. The more she spoke, the easier it became.

Later she wrote, "You must do the thing you think you cannot do."

With Eleanor's help, Franklin became the governor of New York State in 1928.

Franklin's polio had been a challenge for him, but also for Eleanor. Soon she would face an even bigger challenge.

6
The White House

In 1929, the stock market crashed. Millions of Americans lost their jobs. They lost their farms. They lost their homes. They wandered from state to state looking for work. There was no unemployment insurance. There was no money for food. There was hunger. And there was sorrow.

The Great Depression, as this time came to be called, would last for several years.

During this time, Franklin ran for president. Eleanor had mixed feelings, but she supported him. She went with him to Chicago to accept the Democratic party's nomination. Then she traveled by train across the country trying to win votes. She also worked with the women's division of the Democratic party.

In November of 1932, Franklin won the election. Eleanor was now the first lady of the United States. She was facing her biggest challenge yet. Could she keep her independence and help Franklin at the same time? She moved into the White House, secretly dreading the years ahead.

As first lady, Eleanor became Franklin's eyes and ears. She became his legs. She traveled the country inspecting prisons, hospitals, and homes for old people. She lifted the lids on pots to see what people were being fed. She went down into coal mines to see how the workers were treated.

She wanted to know exactly how the people of the nation were getting along. And she told Franklin every detail.

Eleanor serving soup to unemployed women.

Eleanor's energy was astounding. She accomplished more in a day than most people did in a week. People called her "Eleanor Everywhere."

"I learned that true happiness lies in doing something useful with your life," she said.

Eleanor was a popular first lady. In her first year in the White House, she received more than 300,000 pieces of mail!

When Eleanor was a little girl, she had found it hard to make friends. Now she was loved by many. And she was loved for who she was!

7
Eleanor Everywhere

Franklin did not want the country to suffer through a depression ever again. He wanted workers to have unemployment insurance. He wanted old people to have financial security. He wanted young people to have grants so they could stay in school. Franklin called these reforms the New Deal.

Eleanor went on the radio. She spoke about the New Deal. She helped people understand what the president was planning. She also wrote a daily newspaper column. She called it "My Day." The column appeared in papers across the country. Eleanor wrote about the things she saw while traveling around the country. She wrote about what was going on in the White House. The people of the nation saw that someone in government cared about them.

Eleanor broadcasting on the radio.

People also admired Eleanor's courage and sense of adventure. She was the first president's wife to travel by plane. She even flew with Amelia Earhart! The famous pilot wanted people to see that air travel was safe. One evening, after a party in Washington, D.C., Amelia asked Eleanor to fly with her. The two flew from Washington to Baltimore dressed in evening gowns.

"I felt absolutely safe," said Eleanor. "I'd give a lot to be able to fly a plane myself."

People listened to Eleanor. In 1939 the Daughters of the American Revolution refused to let the world-famous black singer Marian Anderson sing at Constitution Hall. Eleanor spoke out against this racial prejudice. She even quit her membership in the organization.

Then Eleanor arranged an even greater concert for Marian Anderson. On Easter Sunday in 1939, the celebrated singer performed a free concert at the Lincoln Memorial in Washington. Seventy-five thousand people came to listen, and millions more heard the concert on their radios.

After the Depression, the Second World War broke out. The United States stayed out of it for a few years. But on December 7, 1941, Pearl Harbor, a naval base in Hawaii, was bombed. The United States was at war!

During the war years, Eleanor visited the troops overseas. She was still Franklin's eyes and ears. She toured the camps in the South Pacific war zone. She spoke to wounded soldiers. She spread humor and hope. She traveled thousands of miles. No one seemed able to keep up with her.

In the fall of 1945, the war ended. But before it did, Franklin Delano Roosevelt died.

UNITED STATES

8
America's Most Admired Woman

Eleanor was now a widow. She thought her public life was over. But she was mistaken. She had one more job to do. President Harry Truman asked Eleanor to attend the first meeting of the United Nations. She was one of five Americans chosen. She was the only woman.

The United Nations is an organization made up of leaders from many nations. It works for worldwide peace. Eleanor and Franklin had always believed that the nations of the world should make peace their common goal.

Eleanor never wanted to see another war. She worked hard for the United Nations. One of the things she did was to help write the Universal Declaration of Human Rights. This document states the rights of every person living on earth. It is now published in every language of the world.

Eleanor Roosevelt was now in her seventies. But she still worked long hours. She kept writing "My Day." She wrote books, lectured, and hosted a weekly television interview show.

Sixteen years after Franklin's death, Eleanor was still considered "America's Most Admired Woman."

Eleanor was finally slowed down by sickness. She went into the hospital for tests. The doctors told her that she had an incurable blood disease.

On her seventy-eighth birthday, Eleanor asked her friends to plan a party for her. She wanted the guests to be children. Even when she was sick, Eleanor was thinking of others. A month later, on November 7, 1962, Eleanor Roosevelt died in her sleep.

Eleanor Roosevelt worked hard for human rights. She worked hard for world peace. She didn't let shyness or fear stand in her way.

"We shape our lives," Eleanor believed. "And we shape ourselves. We are responsible for the choices we make."

Eleanor chose to help others less fortunate than herself. She chose to do what she could to make the world a better place. The shy little girl who wanted to make her father proud had done more than he could ever have imagined.

She had been the first lady of the United States. On her death, Eleanor Roosevelt was called the "First Lady of the World."

Eleanor Roosevelt in her seventies.